Black as Night

by Jacob Funk

Copyright © 2024 by – Jacob Funk – All Rights Reserved.

It is not legal to reproduce, duplicate, or transmit any part of this document in either electronic means or printed format. Recording of this publication is strictly prohibited.

Table of Contents

Acknowledgement i
Dedication ii
About the Author iii
Volume One 1
    Black as Night 2
    Roses 3
    The Garden 4
    My Flesh 5
    Kingdom Come 6
    Finale Part 1 7
    Finale Part 2 8
    Bone 9
Volume Two 10
    Noise 11
    Lost 12
    Petrichor 13
    What I Wasn't 14
    Slowly 15
    Marionette 16
    Think 17
    Shine 18
    Neon Lights 19
    Expansion 20
    Color 21
    Body 22

Acknowledgement

Thank you to everyone who has helped me along the way! A special thank-you to all of my English teachers, who helped nurture my passion for writing.

Dedication

I would like to dedicate this book to Jessica Funk, Sean Brown, and Alen Harvey. As well as Kylen, AJ, Tanner, and Hayden.

About the Author

Jacob is a young author, who's been obsessed with reading and writing since the fifth grade. He started his first book during his summer break going into his junior year of high school.

Volume One

Black as Night

Black as night,
Dark as rain,
Will I always feel this pain?
Black as night,
Cold as ice,
Nothing seems to suffice.
Black as night,
Hard as steel,
None of this seems truly real.
Black as night,
Blinding light,
I want to give up this fight.
Black as night,
Dead as I,
This is where I finally lie.

Roses

Let the roses die,
Where I lie.
Let the tulips pass,
Same as I.
Let the lilies wilt,
And feel not any guilt.
Let the roses die.
Let the roses die.

The Garden

Creeping vines,
twisting lines wrapped around my mind.
Draining weeds make me bleed,
Growing in my soul.
Around my heart,
A garden wall keeping me trapped within.
Around my heart,
An iron wall keeping me trapped in sin.

My Flesh

My brain, my brain,
Filled with pain.
My heart, my heart,
Unkind remarks.
My eyes, my eyes,
See only lies.
My skin, my skin,
Filled with sin.
I tear my skin,
Seam to seam.
I ream my flesh,
My blood is seen.

Kingdom Come

In the land of poetry and prose,
I like to travel where no one goes.
Atop my steed, upon the page,
There is a place I do not age.
A sea of ink and misery,
Not right for you, but just right for me.
In the land of poetry and prose,
There are many places no one goes.
So stay there in your castle walls,
I will watch as your kingdom falls.

Finale Part 1

Goodbye yellow sun lighting up my life.
Goodbye lonely moon lighting up the night.
Goodbye to all the stars,
My most loyal friends.
To all my friends below,
This is where it ends.
And to all the other objects hanging in the sky,
I'll be with you soon,
then us two can fly.
To all those who cared for me
know it's not your fault.
You had no idea how I felt,
my heart was in a vault.
My final words go to you,
So please do not forget.
With all my heart I loved you,
And that I don't regret.

Finale Part 2

I regret not being nice,
I know you feel my heart is ice.
I regret not being better,
The reason you read this letter.
I regret not spreading my love,
But now I'll send it from above.
I regret not being true,
The reason this is what I do.
I regret not doing more,
But now it's time to shut the door.
Bring not any flowers,
Bring not any tears.
We all know this has been coming for years.
So please just let me rot,
And let me be forgot.
That is my final request.
Just let me have peace in death.

Bone

Razor blade cuts,
On the edge of my wrist.
I'm scared, terrified, thinking I can't quit.
I started taking drugs,
To try and numb my mind.
To make my thoughts impossible to find.
I wanted to take the blade,
And cut past the bone.
Living in skin and blood I call my home.
There are names etched deep,
Inside of my mind.
Around and around,
Impossibilities unwind.
Carrying a weight inside of my heart,
Laying in bed,
Hoping everything goes dark.
I'm so alone.
No one to phone.
Forever stuck inside of this zone.
Forced to bear the weight of my sins,
But I'm tired of feeling like I can't win.
I try my best to do no harm,
But yet these scars travel up my arm.

Volume Two

Noise

Loud.
It's so loud.
There's so much noise,
I feel like I'm drowning in the sound.
And time slips away,
Like grains of sand in an hourglass.
Sitting all alone,
Just waiting for the time to pass.
With my eyes transfixed to the clock on the wall.
Tick tock,
Tick tock,
Down I fall.
So much noise,
Like TV static.
My thoughts are all mixed up,
Deep inside it's truly tragic.
I try to pry away from making half-baked thoughts,
Keep them all fully cooked,
With a hollandaise sauce.
But I still have raw emotions,
That I keep inside.
It's all just a product of a weakened mind.

Lost

I got lost again today.
Just like the day,
Week,
Month,
Year before.
And when I think more,
I can't remember the last time I was found.
I can't remember the last time I said something remotely profound,
Because everything I do is for someone else.
All so they can run around and pretend they like me.
But where does the compassion end,
And the guilt begin?
When will my heart feel whole again?
I never know.
Because I've never been given the chance to grow,
To change,
To be good.
They expect perfection,
And when I fail,
I get dashed to the side,
Left in the sleet and hail.
No corrections to my choices,
So I go back to the same voices.
No room for love,
No room for heart,
So I get lost once again.

Petrichor

pet·ri·chor
/ˈpetrī,kôr/
noun
- a pleasant smell that frequently accompanies the first rain after a long period of warm, dry weather.

I always liked the smell of rain.
Someone else did too,
So they gave it a special name.
With rain comes life,
And new beginnings.
It allows me to lose sight of what's in my mind,
And gain sight of what's in front of me.
Because sometimes it's hard to see.
When I'm always on my phone,
Or stuck watching TV.
Or because I'm trapped inside my room,
Afraid that if I leave,
It will spell my doom.
Because it's the only place I feel safe.
I can avoid the noise and strife that comes with life.
And no, I don't really want to die,
But I'm not really living a life, I'm living a lie.
I've always liked the smell of rain.
Maybe I had just hoped it would wash me away.

What I Wasn't.

Honestly, I'm tired of getting my heart played with.
Because even though I'm used to the cold knife of this alone life,
I'm still scared to die,
And I don't know why.
I barely know what goes on inside myself,
Because I feel my pain persist but,
I can't ask for help.
I'm meant to be strong,
And be numb.
But every person I meet gets me under their thumb.
And every step I take,
I feel regret.
So much so that, sometimes, I just want to go back and forget.
Because I so badly wish to change who I was,
And become what I wasn't.

Slowly

I'll love you slowly,
So fast.
I fell so hard,
No chance to look back.
I thought you fell with me,
Straight down off that cliff.
But instead you stayed up top,
While I landed in a ditch.
And I was terrified,
Spinal fracture,
Risked my life.
I don't know what I did,
To deserve all of this pain.
Now I'm sitting all alone,
Just soaking in the rain.
You loved me slowly, so fast.
And I'm chasing your heart again.
And I don't want this to be,
The end.

Marionette

I'm a puppet.
Strings are attached to my hands and my feet.
I'm stuck,
Trapped inside,
Please help, this isn't me.
Honest to god,
In which I don't believe,
Help me, I'm stuck,
Strapped down on this seat.
Looking through these cold eyes.
Feeling like my whole life,
I've been telling bold lies,
Telling people I'm fine.
But really,
I'm about to break down.
Curled up on the floor,
Making terrible sounds.
But my wooden face says something else.
Still attached to these strings,
It's a living hell.
So I stand on the stage, bowing to the applause.
Hoping they see me, through the masks cracks and flaws.

Think

Cogito Ergo Sum.
I think, therefore I am.
But then I started to think about what I think about,
And what I think about is a sham.
Because our world has gotten boring.
We've gotten rid of the pain and strife,
The dark and light that comes with life.
We've forgotten why we fight.
For love, for might.
For our right to write.
And that's why I choose not to die.
Because I started to think about what I think about.
And I think about why we choose to stay alive.

Shine

Nobody's living a life anymore.
Their minds are a bore because their minds are bored.
I wonder what would happen if I got rid of technology.
No more phones, or tablets, or TV.
I think we'd all be a little bit more free.
Free to play, free to fight, free to think, free to love.
Free to run, free to fear, free to be okay with losing that which we hold dear.
We should be okay with losing our mind from time to time.
Otherwise you won't find the time to find your mind in the first place.
And since birth, you've been in a race.
To be the fastest, smartest, strongest.
To be the best.
But nobody takes any time to rest.
Nobody takes any time to show the world it's okay to not constantly shine.
It's okay to not constantly be in the limelight.
You don't need to be a superhero to crime fight.
All you need to do,
Is just be you.

Neon Lights

There is so much light in our world.
Neon signs that fill our minds with distractions.
Preventing us from taking the correct actions.
But if we could see the stars,
If we could see just how small we are,
We'd realize everyone's got scars.
That most people don't have time to bide,
To hide and lie in wait for the right moment.
Because we can't wait for the stars to align,
If we can't see them shining in the sky.
So we're just stuck.
Waiting and watching,
And weighing our words against the power of our actions.

Expansion

The sun is impossibly hot, and space is impossibly cold.
It seems like they could never coexist, being diametrically opposed.
But the sun keeps spinning, and space keeps expanding.
It's almost exactly like you, me, and humanity.
But we've got a lot more bloodshed, gunfights, and insanity.
And it's absolutely astounding just how much we've grown.
But so many people still have no place to call home.
No place inside their heart where they can choose to rest their mind,
And try to find the time to unwind.
Because everything's getting bigger, faster, better, louder.
Trying to find more space to crowd.
But eventually it all breaks down.
The problem with expansion is you need things to fill the space in which you inhabit.
And if you don't have enough things, enough time,
Eventually it all starts to fall apart.
So please tug on that thread.
Tug on those heartstrings.
Take your drum, hit it on or off beat.
Don't fill your space with things that decay.
Fill your space with sounds and colors and ideas
That fills your mind for the rest of time.

Color

The world is losing its color.
Every day, rushing past are flashes of black, white, and gray.
But never blue, green or red.
Every day, every second that passes by, the world becomes more and more dead.
Until eventually, gray is all we have left.
No more sound, art or music.
No more life to rejoice, or stories to regale with people around the campfire, listening to your tale.
Your story filled with life and pain and strife and hate.
No more ways to relate.
Not to ourselves, to our peers.
Because we can't handle someone talking about their fears.
And at some point, you need to realize that it's your life to live,
Your love to give.
And if you can't handle the fact that you need to reach out and make a connection, then give up.
Go home, keep being defective.
Or, get some color in your cheeks, puff out your chest, and find someone to meet.

Body

I hate my body.
Get it through your head.
I hate my body.
Don't want the life I've led.
To many wrist scars,
Body falling apart.
I want you to watch me decay.
Please don't cry, no, it's okay.
I want you to tear it apart.
Plunge into its chest, I beg.
And tear out its heart.
Dig into its brain,
Each neuron.
Throw it away.
My lungs won't help it breathe.
My eyes won't let it see.
My tongue can't make it speak.
Its hands have crippled me.
I hate my mutilated body,
Someone throw it away.
I hate my mutilated body,
Please just let it decay.

www.ingramcontent.com/pod-product-compliance
Lightning Source LLC
Chambersburg PA
CBHW041311110526
44590CB00028B/4320